Joseph Cook's

INVERNESS

First published 1992 by The Inverness Courier
Printed by Highland Printers
© The Inverness Courier

Cover picture: Inverness in 1856

INTRODUCTION

TO MARK the 175th anniversary of The Inverness Courier on December 4th, 1992, we decided to take a pictorial ramble down memory lane.

A ready source of interesting material was to hand, for the Courier had access to the splendid Joseph Cook Collection of photographs, which capture the life and times of the Highland Capital between the 1850s and the 1920s.

As you turn the pages of this book you will remark how much has changed over the years, and not always for the better. The demolition of so many fine old buildings to make way for uninspiring redevelopments has to be a cause for regret.

Joseph Cook (1881-1973), who was a director of Walker's Sawmills, Inverness, took a great interest in his native town and went out of his way to obtain photographs of as many aspects of its past as he could find. It did not matter to him whether a picture had been taken by a professional or an amateur: it was the subject that counted.

Over the years he built up a large collection of photographs, providing a unique record of Inverness in the latter half of the 19th century and the early part of the 20th. For this commemorative book, the Courier has selected some of the best pictures from the valuable Cook archive, including four pre-First World War hand-coloured views. Some of the scenes will probably stir recollections among older sections of the population. And for the younger generation, the whole book will act as a window on a vanished age.

John Macdonald,
Editor,
The Inverness Courier

CONTENTS

Joseph Cook's

INVERNESS

Photographs from The Joseph Cook Collection, courtesy
of the Rev. R.B. Henderson, Inverness
Words by Duncan Ross

Inverness in 1856

ONE of the earliest photographs of Inverness, this view of the riverside is dated 1856, only seven years after floods washed away the old stone bridge which had served the town since 1685.

The suspension bridge which replaced it was opened on 23rd August, 1855, and remained one of the town's most prominent landmarks until it, too, was replaced by the present traffic bridge in 1961.

On the left is the Free High Church, now St Columba's, built only a few years before this picture was taken by Francis Frith, a well-known English photographer of his day.

Apart from the church, the steeple, and the castle, one of the few buildings in this scene still left standing is the Courier Office at the corner of Bank Lane.

The washerwomen of Inverness had a ready bleaching green in the grassy slopes of the river bank.

Thatched cottages in Tomnahurich Street

THE "parish pump" was always a popular meeting place for the exchange of the latest news and gossip.

Tomnahurich Street had two — the East Pump and the West Pump — and local families were charged an annual water rate for their upkeep.

In 1845, when the charge was a shilling a year, a number of local women "conspired to withhold payment" until their pump was put in a better state of repair.

"Unfortunately the pump was the cause of many an untoward incident due to certain housewives demanding priority rights and monopolising the water station to do her week's washing, while her neighbours attacked her in wordy warfare," wrote Joseph Cook.

"Many a threat to bring the matter before the Council was voiced, and the contents of the washtub have been known to have been subjected to unladylike usage."

The cottages are said to have been the last thatched houses in Tomnahurich Street.

Inverness from Tomnahurich

THIS panoramic view of the town, from Tomnahurich, was taken over 100 years ago. The foreground area bounded on the right by Glenurquhart Road and on the left by Bruce Gardens (formerly Cemetery Road) had become a public park by the early 1890s.

In June 1897 it was formally opened by Provost William MacBean as the Victoria Park, complete with bandstand, in honour of Queen Victoria's Diamond Jubilee.

He declared it to be a public park and recreation ground for the people of Inverness "in all time coming", but between the wars the Town Council developed the area for housing.

One of the first streets to be built, Park Road, was originally known as Victoria Park Road. Maxwell Drive, Lindsay Avenue, and Smith Avenue followed later.

High Street and The Exchange

A QUIET town centre scene at the turn of the century, when horse-drawn cabs ruled the cobbled streets and there was no need for pedestrian priority zones.

On the left is the imposing facade of the Bank of Scotland, built in 1848 as the headquarters of the Inverness-based Caledonian Bank.

The Forbes Fountain in the foreground was donated to the town in 1880 by Dr George F. Forbes of Millburn. When The Exchange fell victim to road widening operations, the fountain was dismantled and stored. Unfortunately, some pieces went missing and it was a truncated version which was later re-erected on the riverside near Cavell Gardens.

At the corner of Castle Street, where McDonalds now dispense hamburgers, stands MacKay's Clan Tartan Warehouse. Above it was the YMCA. The building was topped by statues of the "three graces" of Faith, Hope and Charity. Each about 7ft tall, they were the work of Inverness sculptor Andrew Davidson (1841-1925). The statues went into a council depot when the building was demolished in 1955 and were later sold to an Orkney antiques collector.

Dalcross's House, Church Street

THIS venerable house at the corner of Church Street and Queensgate was completed in 1700 for a wealthy Inverness merchant, James Dunbar of Dalcross.

By the mid-19th century it was occupied by tradespeople, although some of the rooms were still said to bear "indications of former grandeur".

This picture was taken shortly before demolition of the building in 1900, to make way for a handsome new block completing the south side of Queensgate. The Church Street end comprised the North of Scotland Bank, later the Clydesdale.

The main block, which included the Queensgate Hotel, was virtually destroyed by fire in May 1992 but the former bank, by then a cafe bar, escaped the worst of the damage.

All that remains of Dalcross's House are the four triangular pediments from the upper windows, one of which was built into the wall above the entrance to the bank.

Gordon Place

THE group of houses here, known as Gordon Place, originally had front gardens sloping down towards the river, but these disappeared when the road was widened and raised in height for the opening of the Suspension Bridge in 1855.

When the houses were demolished in 1900 a number of older stones were found, including a lintel inscribed "1604". They may have come from the town residence of the Robertsons of Inshes, which occupied the site until the end of the 18th century.

Gordon Place was succeeded by the second "Castle Tolmie", a group of larger properties with external stone staircases. The architect was William Carruthers, a grandson of Dr Robert Carruthers, one-time proprietor of the Courier. They came down in 1959 to allow for demolition of the Suspension Bridge and construction of the present bridge, opened in September 1961.

The original "Castle Tolmie", built in 1678, stood on the opposite corner of Bridge Street.

Dunbar's Hospital, Church Street

ONE of the oldest buildings in the town, Dunbar's Hospital dates back over 300 years to Provost Alexander Dunbar, who endowed funds to provide a new "hospital house" for the poor.

A sequence of carvings and inscriptions above the attic dormers includes the figure of a "bedesman" or licensed beggar, the date 1668, and the following text:

"This poor man cryed. And the Lord heard him and saved him out of his tryel. A little that a righteous man hath is better nor the Richis of manye vikid men. Hie that giveth to the poor leneth to the Lord and Hie vill paye them seavens tyms more."

The ground floor, on the right of the entrance, housed the town's Grammar School until 1792, and to the left was a weigh-house. In its day the building also served as a poorhouse, cholera hospital, library, fire station and soup kitchen. At one time the town's gallows was stored upstairs.

The Cheese Market, Inglis Street

THE Martinmas Market was held each year around the end of November and was one of the few open air fairs to survive into the late 19th century.

It was also known as the Cheese Market, as kegs of butter and home made cheeses from the crofts and small farms around the town were the staple produce of the fair.

In its heyday the Martinmas Market occupied most of High Street, Inglis Street and Academy Street, but when this picture was taken in 1888 it had already entered a terminal decline.

As a schoolboy, the young Joseph Cook and his pals had their own way of adding to the merriment of the occasion, however.

"Along with others from the old High School, I can well remember elbowing our way through the crowd and, when occasion offered, pinning together the voluminous skirts of the women as they stood chatting together," he later confessed. "And in those days, skirts were skirts!"

Ness House

BUILT in the 18th century for Colonel John Baillie of Leys, this mansion on Ness Walk became the home of local banker John Mackenzie, later a provost of the town, whose hospitality became a by-word in Inverness society.

"Visitors came to Ness House as freely as they would come to an hotel," a friend recalled. "Invitations were not needed, for an equally hearty welcome awaited every guest whether invited or uninvited.

"On the sideboard in the dining room, refreshments stood ready from morning to night for all comers, while a quaintly-shaped whisky bottle with which to 'speed each parting guest' was a fixture on the entrance hall table."

After Mackenzie's death in 1854 the house was occupied for a while by Royal Engineers engaged in Ordnance Survey work in the Highlands. It was demolished in 1870 to make way for the Palace Hotel.

Near by was a bleaching area known as the Little Green — but the river banks also came in useful on washing day.

The Old High Church

THE parish kirk of Inverness, the Old High, stands on a low hill known as St Michael's Mount, which has probably been in use for Christian worship since the time of St Columba in the 6th century.

The present church, erected in 1769, stands on the site of an earlier building of which only the square tower now remains. It is thought to date from the 15th or 16th century, although the parapet and spire are later additions.

A pre-Reformation church dedicated to the Virgin Mary is recorded on this spot before 1171, but the first church is said to have been established by Columba himself.

After the Battle of Culloden in 1746, Jacobite prisoners are said to have been executed in the churchyard and it is claimed the marks of the musket balls can still be seen on some of the headstones.

Friars Street

ONE of the most attractive pictures in the Joseph Cook Collection, this view of Friars Street was taken around the turn of the century.

It shows the picturesque row of cottages which once lined the street, with the tower of the Old High Church in the background.

On the left is the entrance to Greyfriars Churchyard, the walled burial ground which is all that remains of the Dominican Friary founded by King Alexander II in the 13th century.

The Friary buildings were almost ruinous by 1436, and over two centuries later the stones were sold to Cromwell's army for construction of the Citadel.

Cottages at the Crown

THESE thatched cottages at the Crown, on the corner of Kingsmills Road and Midmills Road, were the last farm buildings in the area to be demolished.

They came down in 1897 to clear a site for the Crown Church, then a United Free congregation, the foundation stone being laid in November 1900.

In the background is the tower of what was then the old High School, now Crown Primary.

St Andrew's Cathedral

COMPLETED in 1869, the Cathedral Church of St Andrew was the masterpiece of Inverness architect Dr Alexander Ross, the "Christopher Wren of the North". As factor to Sir Alexander Matheson of Ardross MP, he was responsible for many of the buildings on the west side of the river.

Ardross Terrace followed in 1873-75, but when this photograph was taken the site of what is now the Tower Hotel was still part of the wooded grounds of Ness House.

It also pre-dates the building of Bishop Robert Eden's residence, Eden Court, in 1876-78.

It was Bishop Eden who decided to move the seat of the diocese from Elgin to Inverness and the foundation stone of the new Episcopal Cathedral — the first in Britain since the Reformation — was laid in 1866.

Although the original plans envisaged spires rising a further 100ft from the top of each tower, the funds available did not match these lofty expectations.

Duff Street

TODAY Duff Street has all but disappeared, but when this picture was taken in the closing years of last century it consisted of about 20 mainly thatched cottages, running from King Street right through to Wells Street.

Among the residents, labourers and tradesmen predominated. But the burgh street directory for that period also lists a couple of grocers, a seaman, a cattleman, a fireman, and a pipemaker rejoicing in the name of Barcoll Carroll.

Duff Street was named after the Duffs of Muirtown, who owned the area as part of their estate. It originally marked part of the western boundary of the medieval burgh but the street has now vanished, apart from a short stretch beside the Thistle Bar. Only the street name survives, at its former junction with Celt Street, to mark the pedestrian entry to the Falconer Court housing development which replaced these cottages in 1980.

The old Town House

INVERNESS Town Council held its meetings on the first floor of this building from the early 1700s until 1878.

"A plain building of rubble," was how Captain Edmund Burt described it in 1754. It could have been a really handsome Council chamber, he remarked, "but the walls are rough, not white-washed or so much as plastered, and no furniture in it but a table and some rough chairs, and altogether immoderately dirty."

The building was originally Lord Lovat's town residence, but it was sold to the Council in 1709 and rebuilt, with later additions in 1750, to form the three-storey building seen here.

The ground floor with its arcade of seven arches contained a public reading room, the Council Chamber was above, and the top floor was used for over a century by the Guildry, which had contributed to the rebuildings costs.

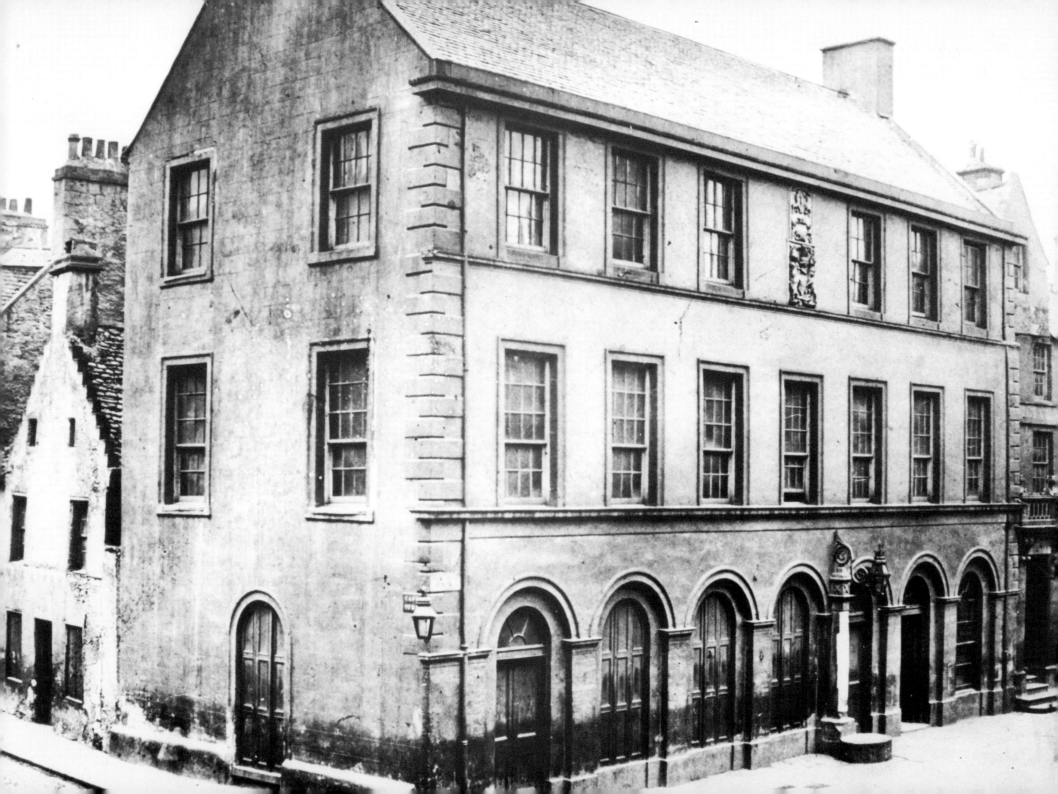

Demolition of the old Town House

IN 1865 the local historian, and later MP, Charles Fraser Mackintosh observed that the old Town House, though a handsome and roomy building, was not strong.

"It ought to be taken down soon, and it would be well for the town to acquire certain neighbouring properties … in order to permit the erection of such extensive and elegant buildings as the convenience of the site, importance of the town, and growing requirements of trade do certainly demand."

The Town Council eventually took his advice, and the building was pulled down in 1878. The new Town House, "an ornate Victorian Gothic edifice", was completed in 1882 and opened by one of Queen Victoria's younger sons, the then Duke of Edinburgh.

MacDougall's Royal Tartan Warehouse, High Street

DONALD MacDougall established his tartan warehouse in the 1840s, but rebuilt it in 1878-79 in the ornate and turreted Baronial style seen here.

The royal arms of Scotland are carved on the central panel above the second floor, and the pend below leads through to Lombard Street. Upstairs is now the Highland Club, while the presence of a mill shop on the ground floor continues the connection with the clothing trade.

The Victorian obsession with Highland dress proved a profitable one for Mr MacDougall, who numbered the Queen and Prince Albert among his customers. Regular orders would arrive from Balmoral and almost every royal court in Europe.

As a successful businessman, he became a notable benefactor to the town. He founded the Working Men's Club in Drummond Street in 1865 and largely financed its move to Bridge Street four years later. Annual payments are still made to local organisations from the MacDougall Trust.

Church Street and Fraser Street

THE Highland gentry and their sporting guests would have been regular customers at both of these Church Street premises.

Morel Brothers of Piccadilly, wine merchants and Italian warehousemen, opened their Highland branch principally to serve the country houses and shooting lodges around Inverness.

But they also found a ready local demand for their range of wines, spirits, and "foreign comestibles of all descriptions". In 1896, having become "Purveyors to the Queen and Royal Family", Morels' moved to Queensgate, beside the Post Office, where they remained until the early 1950s.

W. A. MacLeay and Son supplied everything the discerning sportsman could possibly require, and advertised themselves as the largest taxidermy establishment in Scotland. Birds, animals and fish could be stuffed and, if desired, mounted in glass cases.

Ness railway viaduct

AFTER the severe winter of 1892, the River Ness was in heavy spate and the engineers of the Highland Railway feared for the safety of the railway bridge.

The tremendous force of the water scoured cavities from the river bed, and the piers had to be strengthened by tipping stones into these hollows from railway trucks on the bridge.

The five-arched viaduct was opened on 11th June, 1862, to the design of Joseph Mitchell (1803-83), the town's foremost engineer of the Victorian era. Mitchell's Lane is named after him.

His railway viaduct withstood many another Highland winter, until finally succumbing to the flood waters of the Ness in February 1989. Its replacement, a functional but uninspiring structure, was opened in May 1990.

Crown Football Club

THE game of soccer was slow to reach Inverness, but once here it caught on quickly.

By the mid-1880s, the local "football" clubs were still playing a game we would now call rugby, but on 7th March,1885, a fixture with a difference took place at the Northern Meeting Park between the Crown Club and Nairn County.

"It being the first match played in Inverness under Association rules, it attracted a considerable crowd, who seemed to be favourably impressed with the play." Thus the Courier reported on the town's first soccer match, which ended in a goal-less draw.

After a short period playing both kinds of football, most clubs soon came to concentrate on the Association game and the first organised competition — the Inverness Charity Cup — was instituted later that year.

Among the Crown team pictured here in 1887 are Mr Christie the jeweller and, on the extreme right, Archie MacGillivray. Crown later merged with Union (formerly Ballifeary FC) to form Inverness Thistle.

Rovers Football Club

EACH club had its own territory and Rovers, founded in 1885, drew its players and support from the Harbour area. They played on a ground at Needlefield, on the Longman.

They are pictured in 1887 when the captain was a young man called Murdoch Macdonald. He went on to acquire an international reputation as a consulting civil engineer, particularly for his work on Egypt's Aswan Dam, and as Sir Murdoch Macdonald he served as MP for Inverness from 1922 to 1950.

He was made a Freeman of the town in 1930, at the same time as Ramsay MacDonald and Stanley Baldwin, and died in 1957 in his 91st year.

Also pictured is John C. Mackay, later to become the Courier's chief reporter.

The full team was (left to right): Standing — Mr Dickson, James Fraser, Donald Mackenzie, James Stewart, J. C. Mackay, Evan Macdonald, Edward Shaw; Sitting — J. M. Dickson, William Gibb, Murdoch Macdonald, Murdo Mackenzie, Alex Mackenzie.

North of Scotland 2nd XI Football Association

THE year 1899 seems to have been a successful one for these members of the North of Scotland 2nd XI Football Association.

The occasion is not known, but a report in the Courier of 13th June that year offers a clue:

"In the Muirtown Hotel last night, the North of Scotland 2nd XI Football Assocation presented the Muirtown Challenge Shield to the Nelson FC. Mr James Mackintosh, the president, made the presentation and Miss Morris handed the badges to the successful eleven.

"Later in the evening Mr John MacBean, vice-president, handed the caps to the players in the Association team who took part in the match against Aberdeen."

We must take Joseph Cook's word for it that the line up includes Hugh Ross, later to be a Provost of Inverness.

Others he mentions are Fraser, Mackay, Colville, Lyon, Chisholm, Johnstone, Fotheringham, John McBean, James Mackintosh, and Angus Forbes.

Opening of the new tennis courts at Ballifeary

THE Inverness Tennis Club's new courts in Bishop's Road were opened on 4th June, 1892, by the local MP, Robert Finlay.

"The courts, which are among the finest in the North, have been laid out in excellent style," the Courier reported. "The Tennis Club, which has received a large accession of members, deserve to be congratulated upon the success which has attended their efforts in providing such splendidly equipped ash courts."

An Edinburgh man and a lawyer by profession, Finlay was twice the MP for Inverness Burghs, from 1885-92 and from 1895-1906. During his second term, as Sir Robert Finlay, he was Solicitor General for England and then Attorney General. He served as Lord Chancellor from 1916-18, was created 1st Viscount of Nairn the following year, and later became a member of the International Court of Justice. He died in 1929.

Skating on Loch na Sanais

THERE is a certain Brueghelesque quality to this scene of skaters on Loch na Sanais during the great frost of 1895.

Said to mean "loch of the whispering", one theory is that the loch was created by the extraction of clay for construction of the Caledonian Canal.

It was also used for curling — first introduced to the town in 1838 by Robert Wilson of the Caledonian Hotel — and was the home of Inverness Curling Club for nearly 100 years.

Partially filled in with the opening of Torvean Golf Course, what remains of Loch na Sanais is now a haven for bird life.

Dunain Races

HORSE racing in Inverness dates back at least to the 17th century when there were annual races around the hill of Tomnahurich.

The sport was later transferred to the Longman, under the auspices of the Northern Meeting, and then to Dunain where this picture was taken in 1897. The races continued until about 1914.

"It is a pity that the annual trip to Dunain has gone by the board, even although its effect was not altogether conducive to keeping on an even keel some of the more speculative elements in and around Inverness," wrote Joseph Cook,

"Some will remember well the brakes and cabs, in fact anything on wheels that a horse could draw, all making their way along Tomnahurich Street in the morning. And when the show was over and darkness fell, some could be seen on foot making their way towards Clachnacuddin poorer but wiser men."

Northern Meeting Games

THE Northern Meeting, highlight of the social year for lairds and gentry, held its first official Highland Games at the Longman in 1837.

They proved a turning point in the flagging fortunes of the Northern Meeting and became increasingly popular with the Inverness public, moving to a permanent home with the opening of the Northern Meeting Park in 1864.

The Games enjoyed continued success throughout the first two decades of this century, but in the 1930s attendances began to dwindle and losses grew.

It was decided to cancel the 1939 event when it was found the dates clashed with the Nairn Games, and the outbreak of war a few months later sealed the fate of the Games. They were not revived after the war, along with the balls and piping competitions, and the Northern Meeting Park was sold to the Town Council in 1946.

A group of anglers at Loch Ness

A FISHING expedition to Loch Ness was a major undertaking in the 1860s, involving not only boats and gillies, but the hire of a coach and pair for the journey out from Inverness.

On this occasion the top-hatted coachman and his young assistant joined the party for a souvenir photograph by the loch-side.

It was presumably taken before the day's sport commenced, for there is no sign of any fish.

But as Joseph Cook observed: "Each and all would have added their quota to that long and somewhat untrustworthy list of fishing stories, without which the sport would be a very uncolourful and matter-of-fact affair."

Grouse beaters, Moy Estate

IN late August 1911, King George V was a shooting guest of the Mackintosh of Mackintosh at Moy Hall.

During his four days on the grouse moors the sport was said to have been excellent, and the King's party — nine guns in all— bagged a total of 1400 brace.

The success of the visit would have been due in no small measure to this army of beaters recruited from the estate.

An Inverness schooner

THE Inverness schooner Margaret Reid, westward-bound through the Muirtown Locks of the Caledonian Canal.

The photograph was taken about 1884 when the Inverness sailing fleet, which only a few years earlier had numbered between 30 and 40 ships, was starting to decline.

As Joseph Cook put it, the "poetry of natural movement" had begun to give way to the demands of steam, and the once-thriving shipbuilding industry in Inverness had already come to a halt.

Born and brought up in Shore Street, and a member of Inverness Harbour Trust for more than 50 years, Cook took a lifelong interest in the maritime heritage of his home town and the adventures of its hardy seafarers.

The Margaret Reid was skippered by a Captain A. MacLean, who may be one of the figures seen on deck.

The Regent and The Progress

THE Caledonian Canal was blocked for three weeks in April 1881 when these two schooners wedged themselves together in the sealock at Clachnaharry, hung in mid-air for a while as the tide went out, then crashed in a tangled heap to the bottom.

It was the practice for ships of that size to pass through the Canal in pairs, but it soon became obvious that on this occasion the lock was too narrow for them both.

The Inverness-registered Regent was bound for Cardiff with a cargo of potatoes, while the Progress, from Castletown, Isle of Man, was carrying coal to be discharged at Muirtown.

Damage to both vessels was not as bad as originally thought and they were able to be salvaged and repaired. The photograph may have been taken for insurance purposes.

Schooner, Kessock Roads

AT one time Inverness was the home port of between 30 and 40 vessels, trading with Leith, Tyneside, Europe, the Baltic and beyond.

Local shipyards included Munro's and MacGregor's, on the Merkinch side of the river, and Cook's and Stewart's on the Shore side.

Grant Street and Anderson Street were named after rival firms of sailmakers, and there were rope works in Rose Street and on what later became Caley's Telford Street ground.

Shipbuilding came to a halt about 1880 with the rise of steam power, and by the 1930s Joseph Cook was paying homage to "a fleet of white-winged craft that has gone from the seas for ever."

This atmospheric study of a schooner at anchor in the late evening was captioned: "A Shadowy Ship on a Glittering Sea".

The nameless vessel, in the approach to Inverness harbour, is a fine example of what Cook called "the beauty, the grace, and even the mystery which hung around every craft which disappeared across the horizon under a full head of sail".

Inverness Harbour

A BUSY scene at Inverness Habour in the 1880s or 1890s. "Steam and sail are working side by side, as sea transport was then in its transition stage," wrote Joseph Cook.

"Centuries ago Inverness kept up a trade with the Continent and was a town of considerable importance. If it were not for the River Ness and its port, Inverness would today be of very little consequence."

He recalled with nostalgia the days when the Merkinch and the Shore were peopled by sailors, ships' carpenters, sailmakers, blacksmiths, and the other tradesmen required by the town's small but thriving shipbuilding industry:

"... when the smell of the hot pitch and archangel tar wafted along the river, when sails were spread on the Capel Inch and the old Ramparts, and the thud of the adze and the rap of the ship carpenter's mallet rang out across the water."

Schooners at the harbour

THIS view of the harbour at Shore Street dates from about the turn of the century, after the wet dock had been filled in.

Formed from part of the moat of Cromwell's Citadel, the wet dock used to be on the left in the foreground of the picture.

It disappeared during a harbour extension, but Joseph Cook could remember when it was so full of ships that the boys of the Shore could clamber over the closely-packed vessels from one side of the dock to the other.

"At the end of the dock was the old gridiron on which the ships requiring repair and caulking were placed and, as this work was tidal, very often during the sma' hours the silence was broken by the sound of caulking mallets, and the flickering light from the fires which heated the pitch pots would dance along the windows of the surrounding houses."

HMS Briton

ORIGINALLY named HMS Brilliant, this former frigate was launched at Deptford in 1814 — just nine years after the battle of Trafalgar.

In 1860, having seen "several naval engagements", she was stripped of her masts, roofed over, and fitted out as a drill ship for the Royal Naval Reserve.

The eight 32-pounders on the lower deck were used for gun practice, while the upper deck was used for cutlass, sword, and pistol exercises.

The Brilliant was based in London, Aberdeen and Dundee before being moved to Inverness in 1876. Renamed HMS Briton 13 years later, she also served for a while as a floating barracks for the militia.

The ship remained berthed at the Muirtown Basin until the Admiralty sent her to the breaker's yard in 1908.

The memory of the Briton lives on, however, as the name of the Inverness Sea Cadets' headquarters in South Kessock.

The convict ship Success

THIS seagoing museum piece had been a popular tourist attraction in Hobart, Tasmania, for nearly 20 years when her enterprising owners sailed her to Britain in the early 1900s.

Reputedly built in 1787 — the year the First Fleet sailed to colonise Australia — the hulk had lain off Melbourne Harbour for years until the Tasmanians spotted her potential.

They fitted her out with dummy convicts and a fearsome collection of balls, chains, handcuffs and fetters. The armour worn by the bush-ranger Ned Kelly was also on display.

The Success spent several weeks in Inverness during the British tour, and many townsfolk paid to see round her at the Muirtown Basin. Her signwriter, it should be noted, had a sense of humour.

Returning to Australia, she was taken to Sydney. But the memory of her past was still too painful and one night she was scuppered at her moorings by persons unknown.

Militia Colour Party

THE Inverness Militia was raised by Sir James Grant of Grant in 1802 and recruited from the counties of Inverness, Banff, Moray, and Nairn.

The regiment received its Colours in 1803 and the following year was numbered the 10th Militia.

During the Napoleonic Wars it served on garrison duty throughout Britain, returning to Inverness in 1814 to be disembodied. Thereafter it was called out periodically for training.

The Militia was re-embodied during the Crimean War and in 1855 it was redesignated the 76th Highland Light Infantry Militia. At the same time the Master of Lovat became the commanding officer, and the uniform became Highland dress with kilts of Hunting Fraser tartan.

The Militia Barracks in Telford Street were built in 1856 to house the permanent staff and stores.

This picture, taken at the barracks, shows the Colour Sergeants in 1877.

The Bannockburn Shield

THE Volunteer movement in the Highlands produced some of the best shots in the country, and competition was fierce among the various companies.

This handsome trophy, depicting scenes from the Battle of Bannockburn, was designed by Major William Gostwyck-Gard of the 91st Highlanders, who was adjutant of the Inverness Highland Rifle Volunteers.

The first competition took place on the Longman ranges at Inverness in September 1882, when the shield was the main prize at the Highland Rifle Association's annual meeting. But the trophy itself was not delivered by the Edinburgh makers until the following January.

The first holders were the Inverness Company and the picture may be of them, or a subsequent winning team, with Maj. Gostwyck-Gard.

Originally called the Northern Counties Challenge Shield, the trophy was renamed when the competition was opened to Volunteer companies throughout Scotland. It is still competed for annually among all branches of the services in Scotland.

The Volunteers

IN the 19th century the Volunteer movement enjoyed considerable support in Inverness, and this group of officers and NCOs includes two provosts of the town.

The central figure is Colin Lyon Mackenzie, provost from 1855-67, and from 1873-75. The bearded officer, second from the right, is Henry Cockburn MacAndrew who held office from 1883-89.

Knighted in 1887, MacAndrew was a leading solicitor in Inverness and a founder of the law firm MacAndrew and Jenkins. According to Joseph Cook, he had a good sense of humour which, in view of the following, is perhaps just as well.

On one occasion a woman client had called to see him about an impending court appearance. Rising to go, she wrapped her shawl firmly about her and turned to him. "Now, Bailie, what I've told you is the Gospel truth," she insisted. "Of course, there'll be lies to be told at the court, but I'm leaving that with yourself."

Highland Volunteer Artillery

OFFICERS of the Highland Volunteer Artillery, pictured in 1901 outside what was then the Farraline Park School (originally Dr Bell's).

Joseph Cook recalled the colourful spectacle of the Artillery Volunteers, in their splendid blue and red uniforms, clattering around the streets of Inverness on a Saturday afternoon.

The horse-power was provided by animals whose weekday duty was to deliver the coal, and the poor beasts had to work overtime to pull the heavy field guns across the Rose Street bridge.

On the downward slope they would break into a trot and "the rattle of the axles could be heard throughout the district".

Any drop in recruitment was a cause for concern, and it is said that Colonel Baillie of Dochfour helped to secure the Grant Street Park for Clachnacuddin FC in the 1890s in return for a promise of support from the young men of the Merkinch.

1st Inverness-shire Rifle Volunteers

IN the late 1850s and early 1860s, renewed friction between Britain and France sparked off a wave of patriotism and led to the formation of many new Volunteer regiments — forerunners of today's Territorial Army.

Initially they were raised as independent companies, with differing uniforms, but gradually they came under greater central control.

Seven companies were raised in Inverness, Lochaber, Badenoch and the Aird between 1859 and 1861, and three more followed in Portree, Ardersier and Roy Bridge.

In 1880 they were consolidated as the 1st Inverness-shire (Inverness Highland) Rifle Volunteers, and the uniform for all companies became a red doublet with buff facings and kilt of the 42nd or "Government" tartan.

This picture of the Volunteers on parade in Farraline Park dates from around that time.

In 1883 the battalion became the 1st Volunteer Battalion, The Queen's Own Cameron Highlanders.

The Lovat Scouts

THE first contingent of Lovat Scouts to return from the Boer War arrived at Inverness Station from Southampton on 14th August, 1901.

They came home to an ecstatic welcome from the people of the town, and in a ceremony on the Exchange every one of them — about 160 officers, NCOs and men — was presented with the Freedom of the Burgh by Provost William MacBean.

The Scouts had been raised the previous year by Lord Lovat, who remained in South Africa with a second contingent, and in 15 months of campaigning had "thrashed the Boers every time".

The band of the Cameron Highlanders had marched the Scouts, "with their bronzed faces and well-knit frames", in triumph from the station.

"Waiting relatives grasped the hands of their returned 'boys' and, at the Exchange, wives, mothers and sisters, unable to restrain their emotion, kissed and embraced the lads, for the dangers they had passed."

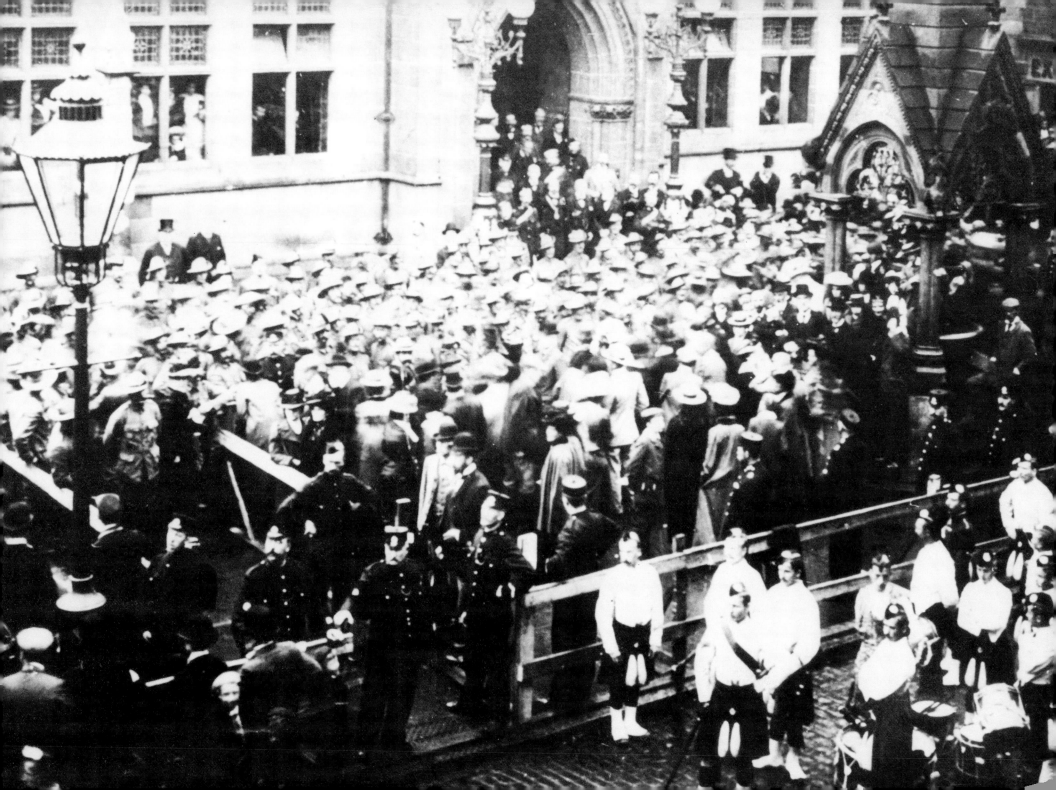

The 4th Camerons march to war in 1914

THIRTEEN years later, almost to the day, Inverness witnessed the departure of the 4th Battalion, The Queen's Own Cameron Highlanders, for the battlefields of France.

The Territorials mobilised at Inverness on the day war broke out, August 4th, 1914, and are seen here in Academy Street in what was to prove to be, for some, the last parade through their home town.

The battalion moved first to Cromarty, to protect the Invergordon Naval base, and then headed south for training at Bedford with the Seaforth and Cameron Brigade of the Highland Territorial Division.

The 4th Camerons were up to strength and were warned for an early move to France, but an epidemic of measles delayed their departure until early the following year.

They arrived on the Western Front in France, 960-strong, on February 20th, 1915. Their first major action was the attack on Neuve Chapelle, in which the battalion suffered 140 casualties.

Station Square

THE Cameron Monument in Station Square was a recognised cab stance and departure point for excursions to places of interest around the town.

This picture must have been taken in or after 1898, because in that year the entrance to the Station Hotel was moved from Academy Street to the corner beside the station.

Around that time the manager was Edward Cesari, and the hotel was able to boast in its advertisements: "Patronised by their Royal Highnesses the Prince and Princess of Wales, and other members of the Royal Family, and by most of the Nobility of Europe."

Like most of the big hotels at that time, it had uniformed porters to await the arrival of the trains, and an "omnibus" was provided to take guests to and from the canal steamers at Muirtown Locks.

The hotel itself was built in 1859, but does not now possess its handsome dome.

Inverness Station

A NOSTALGIC look back at the steam age, in the heyday of the Highland Railway. On the right is the famous Lochgorm Locomotive Works, built in 1864 on the site of a lochan of that name. Carriage and wagon shops were later built at Needlefield, on the Longman.

The first sod for the Inverness & Nairn Railway was cut by the Countess of Seafield on 21st September, 1854, in a field to the east of Millburn House. A public holiday was declared, and over 8000 people turned out to watch the ceremony. The line was opened just over a year later, on 5th November, 1855.

In 1861 it merged with the Inverness & Aberdeen Junction Railway and, following further amalgamations with lines to the north and south, the Highland Railway was born in 1865. Its headquarters remained in Station Square until the Highland became part of the London Midland & Scottish Railway in 1923.

Station platform, Inverness

RIVAL railway companies also had offices in the town, and notice boards on Highland Railway platforms, but they all lost their separate identities with the amalgamations of the 1920s.

Joseph Cook told the story of two farmers travelling home from market after a few drams. "This amalgamation's a grand thing," said one. "I'm going to Muir of Ord and you're going to Keith, and the one train does us fine."

They should perhaps have checked the timetable with Inverness station superintendent William Forbes, the top-hatted figure in this picture from the 1880s or 90s.

He was station master at Grantown West before moving to Inverness on the death of his predecessor, George Critchley.

Forbes was remembered as a large, bearded man "of boundless energy and enthusiasm, who was completely devoted to his work and always ready to lend a hand where needed."

This patriarchal figure was in his 90s when he died.

Locomotive "Raigmore" c. 1869

THE first railway in the north, between Inverness and Nairn, was opened in 1855, but for the first four years of its existence it ran in splendid isolation from any other line.

All the heavy plant and machinery for the new railway had to come by sea, including the four tender engines ordered from Hawthorns of Leith by William Barclay, the company's first locomotive superintendent.

Built between 1855 and 1857, they were numbered 1 to 4 and named after the residences of railway directors — No 1 "Raigmore", No 2 "Aldourie", No 3 "St Martins" and No 4 "Ardross".

Originally they had no cabs and offered very little protection to the engine men. But "Raigmore" and "Aldourie" were extensively rebuilt about 1869 by Barclay's successor, William Stroudley, who is probably one of the figures in the photograph. "Raigmore" was scrapped a few years later but "Aldourie" remained in service until 1899.

Highland Railway snowplough

THE wild and windswept terrain covered by the Highland Railway made it particularly vulnerable to the ferocious blizzards which can strike the North.

Snow fences proved inadequate and during the 1860s snowploughs were developed in three different sizes.

This photograph from 1866 shows the first of the large ploughs, designed and built by William Stroudley at the Needlefield carriage and wagon shops in Inverness.

It was used on drifts of 10ft to 12ft deep. Three or four engines would be coupled together, and the plough would charge at full speed into the snow from about half a mile away. The side flaps were hinged and could be folded up when not in use, to give the driver a clear view of the line ahead.

Stroudley, who was locomotive engineer from 1865-69, is admiring the result of his efforts from the running board of locomotive No 21, built in 1863 and originally named "Forres".

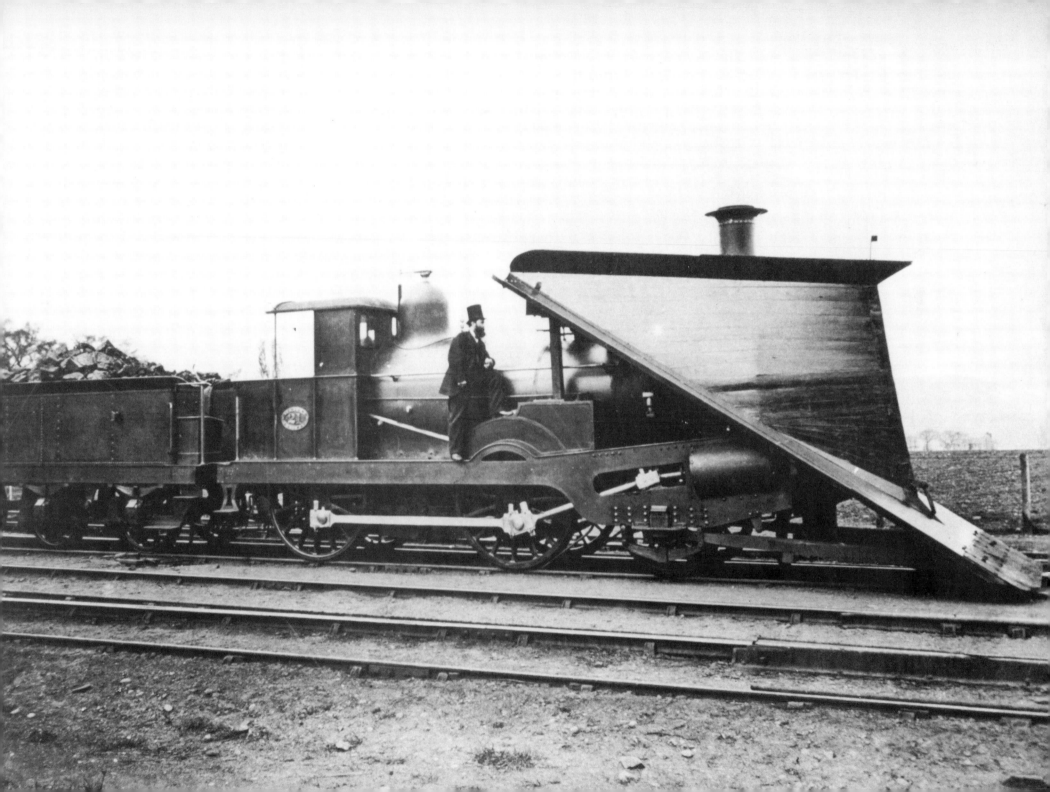

The Baddengorm disaster

THE worst disaster in the history of the Highland Railway occurred in June 1914 when the swollen waters of the Badden Burn swept away a bridge between Aviemore and Inverness — as the northbound train from Glasgow was trying to cross.

After a freak hailstorm there had been an ominous "roaring in the hills" and the burn was soon in raging spate. It carried away a small wooden bridge, which jammed in a narrow gorge. The "dam" then burst sending a wall of water, trees and boulders crashing down on the railway bridge.

Five people died, and news of the tragedy stunned the North. The Courier published an extra edition with the latest details, and James Barron Jr, son of the editor, was despatched to Carrbridge with his camera. The photographic coverage — rare for the Courier in those days — was itself an indication of the gravity of the event.

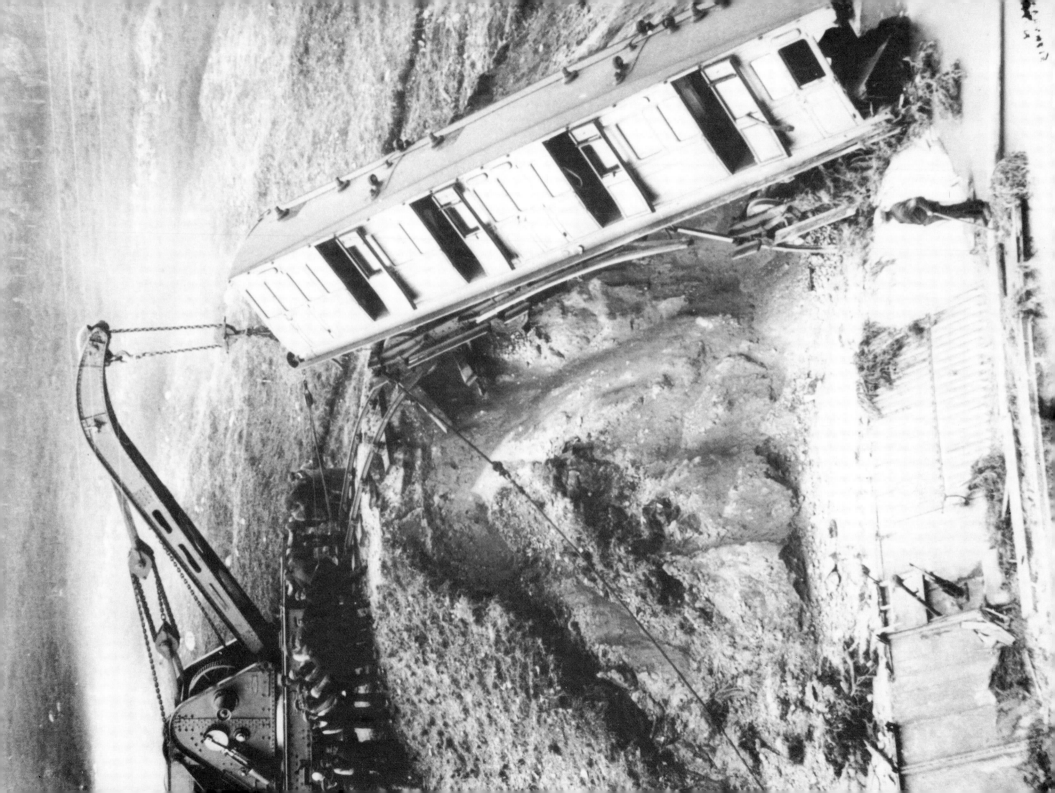

Railway paint shop

INVERNESS did not wait for the railways to reach the Highlands from the south, but vigorously promoted its own schemes.

The driving force behind railway development in the North was the Inverness civil engineer Joseph Mitchell, who had worked with Thomas Telford on road construction in the North.

In 1845 he put forward a bold scheme for which he was ridiculed — a direct line across the mountains to Perth, reaching a height of 1484ft above sea level at Drumochter Pass.

During a Parliamentary debate on Mitchell's plan, an opponent compared it to Hannibal's crossing of the Alps, but his dream was eventually realised in 1863 with the opening of the line via Forres.

The Highland Railway, with its headquarters and locomotive works in Inverness, was one of the biggest employers in the town. Here is the staff of the paint shop, responsible for the upkeep of the company's famous green livery.

Money to burn

INVERNESS in the latter part of the 19th century was arguably a town of even greater importance than it is now.

Not only was it the commercial and administrative hub of the Highlands, as it remains today, it was also the home of two great institutions whose influence on the development and prosperity of the town and the North it is difficult to overstate — the Highland Railway and the Caledonian Bank.

From time to time these twin pillars of the local economy would join together in a solemn ceremony in one of the darker recesses of the railway complex — to burn badly soiled banknotes in the coke oven.

"Unfortunately some of the directors were always present at the ceremony," complained Joseph Cook. "But an old railway employee told me they used to watch the top of the chimney stack, to see if an odd pound note would come out unscathed."

Free Church General Assembly

IN May 1888 the General Assembly of the Free Church of Scotland was held in Inverness, in a specially constructed wooden hall on the riverside at Ness Walk.

The editor of the Courier, James Barron, had a hand in the arrangements and helped to choose the site, where two years later the Palace Hotel was built.

The Moderator that year was the Rev Dr Gustavus Aird, who was made a Freeman of the Burgh in honour of the occasion.

The precentor was Inverness singing master W. S. Roddie who is said to have introduced the novel practice, followed at subsequent Assemblies, of standing up to sing.

It was the second Free Church Assembly to be held in the town. The first occasion was in August 1845, only two years after the Disruption, when a pavilion for 3300 people was erected in Farraline Park, and the classrooms of Dr Bell's School were used as offices.

Cameron Monument

THIS local landmark in Station Square honours the memory of the officers and men of the Queen's Own Cameron Highlanders who died in Egypt and the Nile campaign between 1882 and 1887.

It had been planned to erect a memorial on the esplanade of Edinburgh Castle but it was switched to Inverness "in deference to the wishes of Provost Sir Henry MacAndrew and the Town Council".

The money was raised by serving and former Cameron Highlanders of all ranks, and the site was donated by the Highland Railway.

A sketch of the original design shows a huge obelisk, surmounted by a Sphinx and surrounded by massive ornamental railings, but this was presumably rejected as being too big for the Inverness site.

Instead, the London sculptor George Wade was commissioned to produce the now familiar statue of a Cameron Highlander. The monument, in white Portland stone, was unveiled by Cameron of Lochiel in July 1893.

Reform Bill demonstration

THERE were demonstrations throughout the country when, in 1884, the House of Lords blocked Gladstone's Reform Bill extending the vote to a further two million people.

In September that year about 20,000 people took part in, or turned out to support, a protest march through the streets of Inverness.

Virtually every section of the community was represented, from farm labourers and tradesmen to lawyers and accountants.

Here the printers, lithographers and bookbinders of Inverness are pictured outside the Courier Office before marching off to take part in one of the biggest political demonstrations the town has seen.

On the left, holding the horse for the "printer's devil", is the Courier's editor, James Barron, and beside him is the overseer, Mr Stewart.

Their banners included the emblem of the Typographical Association of Scotland.

Parade of Scouts

SCOUTING in Inverness can be traced back to 1908, the year the movement began to take off in England following publication of Baden Powell's "Scouting for Boys".

The first troop in the town was formed within months of the book appearing and it numbered over 100 by the time of the founder's visit to the Highland Capital in September 1911.

On that occasion a rally was held in the Northern Meeting Park at which over 600 boys from all over the north gave a demonstration of their Scouting skills.

This picture may show one of the contingents marching to that event, or it may have been taken at either of the subsequent rallies in 1912 and 1913.

A second troop, linked to Inverness Cathedral, was formed in 1912 but both troops folded with the outbreak of the First World War and were not revived for many years thereafter.

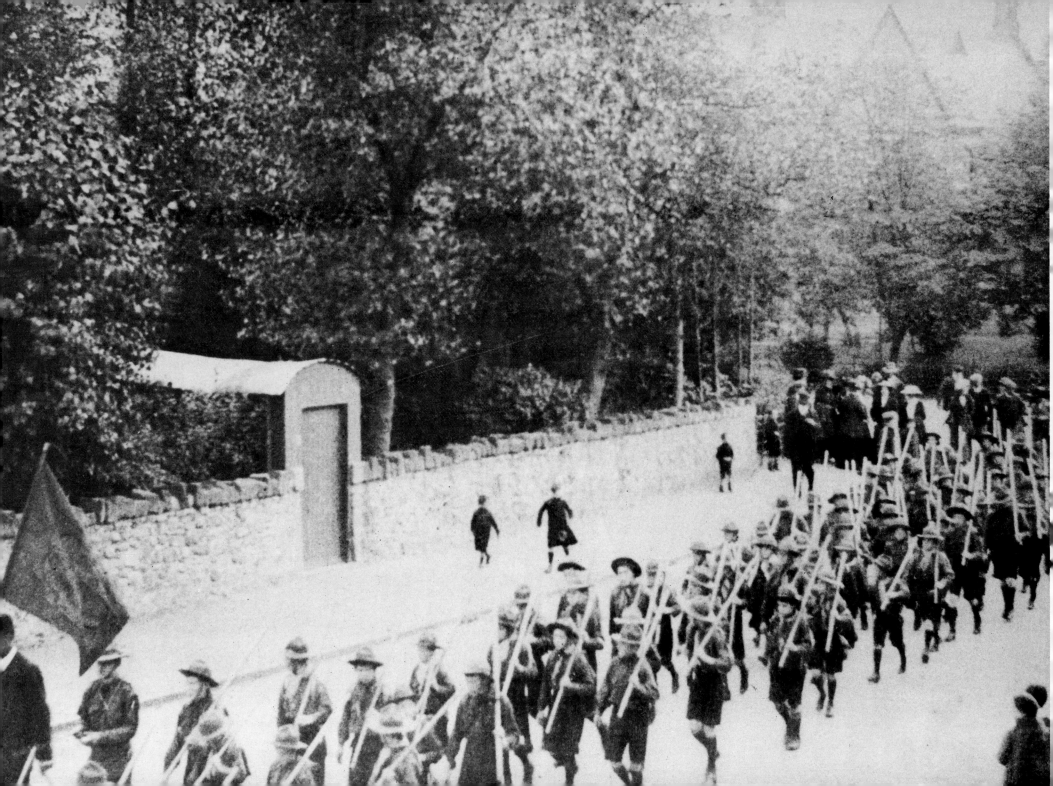

High Street procession

THERE seem to have been more parades and processions in the Inverness of a century ago, and they certainly brought a welcome splash of colour to the town.

The reason for this one is something of a mystery, but it dates from shortly before the turn of the century.

The top-hatted figure on horseback at the front is the Burgh's Chief Constable, J. M. MacDonald, but nothing further is known.

One suggestion is that the occasion was the presentation, in 1897, of an illuminated address to Major-General Sir Hector MacDonald. The Black Isle boy, who joined the Army as a private soldier and rose through the ranks, was very much a local hero.

His first job was as a draper's apprentice in Mackay's Clan Tartan Warehouse, on the corner of Castle Street. The shop has hung out a flag for this parade, so it may have had special cause for celebration.

Edwards Court

RODERICK MacRae and William Dick founded their horse and cab hire business in 1878, offering "first-class open or closed carriages, landaus, wagonettes, transport carts, phaetons, dog carts and gigs."

Their first "posting establishment" was set up in Edwards Court, off Academy Street near the station.

This was behind the house on the left, built by Sheriff-substitute Edwards in 1812 on the site of an old brewery. In more recent times it has been a furniture shop and a restaurant. On the right is the Wesleyan Church, later Stewart's Restaurant.

In the Inverness of Joseph Cook's boyhood, the cab was used for many different purposes.

"On a morning you might see one driving to the cattle sales with a calf tied in a sack, its head protruding under the cabman's legs on the 'dicky'. And an hour or two afterwards he would be driving a bride to the Cathedral or the High Church."

Bunchrew Smiddy

BUNCHREW is reputed to have been the haunt of highwaymen in the 18th century and as late as 1850 there were tales of body-snatching from the near-by churchyard at Kirkton.

By the end of last century, however, losing a horseshoe was probably the worst mishap that could befall a traveller — and the blacksmith was on hand to carry out roadside repairs.

The smiddy, long demolished, was opposite the Mission Church in Bunchrew and within living memory was run by a man called MacRae. His sister, "Jess the Smith", lived in a cottage next door where she sold bread and paraffin for many years.

In addition to shoeing horses and mending the plough, the smiddy was the place to discuss all the important issues of the day, recalled Joseph Cook. "But the horse has been turned off the road, and in many places the ring of the anvil has been silenced for ever."

Dr James Macnee

ONE of the last of the "old school" of family doctors in Inverness, Dr James Macnee was born in 1838 in Tyndrum, Perthshire.

After qualifying at Edinburgh University he practised at Munlochy before moving to Bridge Street, Inverness, during the 1860s.

Dr Macnee became president of the Inverness Medical Society and was also on the staff of the Northern Infirmary.

One of his closest friends was the Rev Dr John Black, Minister of the Free High Church, where Dr Macnee was an elder for many years. It is thought he took this picture of the doctor, while his brougham and coachman stood ready to take him to his next call.

A few years before his death a serious carriage accident had left him permanently lame.

Described as a quiet, kindly, unassuming man, whose fine character and religious faith endeared him to a wide circle of friends, Dr Macnee died in April 1900.

Pioneers of motoring

THREE of the first cars ever seen in Inverness are shown in this photograph taken at the Longman in 1903 or 1904.

They all belonged to local GP Dr George England Kerr, pictured (extreme right) with his medical partners and drivers.

Although never a driver himself, Dr Kerr is credited with — or perhaps it should be blamed for — introducing the motor car to Inverness in the closing years of last century.

His first car was the one in the centre with the tiller steering, but when vehicle registration became compulsory a few years later he was beaten to the record books by five other owners, and his trail-blazing machine — an Arrol Johnstone — was numbered ST6.

Beside Dr Kerr in ST8 is driver Whyte. At the tiller of ST6 is Dr Brown. On the left, driver Cameron is behind the wheel of ST7 beside Dr Nicolson.

Dancing bear

STREET theatre, as it would now be called, has made something of a comeback with the return of High Street and Inglis Street to the pedestrian.

But travelling bands of entertainers, musicians and showmen were a familiar sight in the streets of Inverness in the 1880s and 90s.

The performing bear seen here at the top of Castle Street was a regular visitor and always drew a crowd, although the younger spectators are keeping a respectful distance.

These "actors of the road", as Joseph Cook called them, at one time included an American negro, arrayed in silk top hat and astrakhan-trimmed coat, whose sole ambition in life was to purify the blood of the Highland people with a tonic called Sasparilla.

"While haranguing the people of the town that he wanted no profit, his assistant was doing good business among a good-sized crowd, with a pink-coloured liquid at one shilling a bottle."

The Wool Fair

WHILE sheep and wool were traded in the local hotels, the riverside at Bank Street was the place for buying and selling horses during the annual Inverness Wool Fair.

This lively scene, outside the Courier Office, was photographed before the turn of the century.

The origins of the Wool Fair go back to the Highland Clearances and as an Inverness "institution" it pre-dates the Courier by a matter of months. The first Sheep and Wool Market was held in June 1817 and lasted only one day.

The Courier's subsequent rival, The Inverness Journal (which folded mid-century), reported: "The number of gentlemen interested in sheep farming who attended from the Northern Counties was very considerable. Our flocks are so rapidly on the increase that we understand that there is in Sutherlandshire alone not less than 100,000 Cheviot".

Today the trading of horses is the only aspect of the old Wool Fair to have survived.

Inglis Street parade

STREET parades of all kinds were more common a century ago than they are today, and here the men of the burgh Fire Brigade are cutting quite a dash in their gleaming brass helmets as they march proudly down Inglis Street.

The occasion is not known but, whatever the reason for the parade, it attracted the inevitable escort of excited schoolboys.

Noble & Dreghorn were cabinetmakers and upholsterers whose shop, known as The White House, later became MacPherson's Sporting Stores.

Inglis Street was named after Provost William Inglis, a merchant and banker who was the driving force behind the building of Inverness Steeple and the Northern Infirmary.

It seems to have given some difficulty to the compilers of early Inverness street directories, however. "The houses and shops on the east side of Inglis Street are all wrong numbered," one of them complained. "The numbers are going forward in a backward direction."

High School girls

FIFTH year girls from Inverness High School, pictured about 1875 when the school was in Ardconnel Street opposite what is now the Blind Institute.

Built in the 1840s as the Free Church Institution, the High School was taken over by the Burgh School Board in 1872. Within a few years it moved to the Crown, merging with Raining's School in 1894.

When the present High School was opened in 1937, the younger pupils stayed behind to form the nucleus of Crown School.

The teacher in the background is the English master John E. Finlayson, who went on to become headmaster of Farraline Park School from 1877-97.

It was said that Bible knowledge and honourable conduct counted for more than educational attainment with Mr Finlayson, and he never lost an opportunity to "train his pupils for the battle of life by instilling the sound principles of morality and religion".

Royal Scots Greys

THIS famous cavalry regiment was the star attraction at the Northern Meeting Games around the turn of the century, and they made an imposing sight as they turned from the riverside into Ardross Street.

Small boys everywhere love a parade, and it is tempting to think one of the youngsters trying to march at the head of the column might be the subject of the following story.

A friend of Joseph Cook's was travelling in Egypt and happened to call at a police station to take shelter from a storm. He started chatting with the the chief officer and soon discovered he came from Inverness.

"How in the world did you land out here?" the friend enquired.

"When I was a young man, I went to see the Greys at the Northern Meeting Games," the man replied. "And before I left the field I had joined the cavalry."

The Fire Brigade

THE first proper Fire Brigade in Inverness was established by a worried Town council in 1846 after a spate of destructive fires.

Until then fire-fighting had been the responsibility of the burgh constables, but in March that year an outbreak at the Athenaeum Buildings, opposite the Town House, began to show up deficiencies in the service.

The "very inefficient state of the police" was criticised, and the fire engines were said to be "in wretched order".

In October it was resolved the town should have a proper brigade of trained firemen, under a suitably qualified and experienced superintendent, and by the end of the year a brigade of 18 men had been recruited.

Runners were also paid to bring buckets of water to a fire, with an extra reward of six shillings for the first to reach the scene.

Here the brigade of about 100 years ago pose proudly beside their horse-drawn fire engines.

School fashions

AN interesting study in school fashions from the early days of Inverness High School. The picture dates from the 1870s, when the school was still in Ardconnel Street, before moving to the Crown.

The headmaster at that time was Thomas Wallace. "Not only was he successful as a teacher but his zeal for research into old Inverness and Highland history brought him to the forefront," wrote Joseph Cook. "He was one of the stalwarts of the Field Club in its earlier days, and for a period he looked after the museum."

In 1937 the High School moved west of the river and became known for a time as the Technical High School.

Cook claimed to speak for many former pupils when he complained: "The change of name is against all tenets of tradition and is met with much disfavour and disapproval by those who received their early education under its old and dignified name."

The Music Hall, Union Street

FOR nearly 60 years the Music Hall in Union Street was one of the foremost venues in Inverness for a wide range of entertainments and public meetings.

Choral concerts, musical soirees, pantomime, opera, variety shows, serious plays, lectures and political rallies — the Music Hall took them all in its stride.

Opened in 1865, it could seat 1300 and was intended to cater mainly for visiting artistes, but local amateur groups made good use of it from the outset. Here we see the Northern Amateur Operatic Society, in the early years of the century, with a production of "Yeomen of the Guard".

The Music Hall had been renovated after a serious fire in 1898, and went on to host the National Mods of 1903 and 1912.

It was sold to the Methodists in 1922 and served as their church until another fire destroyed the building in December 1961.

Inverness Choral Union

THE Choral Union was another amateur group which attracted enthusiastic audiences to the Music Hall during the Edwardian era.

Like the Operatic Society, it achieved its large local following under the leadership of W. S. Roddie (sitting centre left, with baton) whose enormous contribution to the musical life of Inverness is still remembered.

A Glasgow man, Stewart Roddie came to Inverness during the 1880s to teach singing at the Royal Academy. He also worked with other local schools and choirs, and as his reputation grew he became well known throughout the Highlands.

He is said to have introduced the sol-fa notation to choirs in the North, and became known as "the man who made the Highlands sing".

Mr Roddie also conducted the choir of the Free High Church (later St Columba High).

Queen Victoria's Diamond Jubilee

THE Diamond Jubilee of Queen Victoria in June 1897 was the cue for a nationwide outpouring of devotion to the Crown in which Inverness proudly played its patriotic part.

Four pages of the Courier were given over to a minutely detailed report of the day's celebrations and the decorations which festooned almost every building in the town.

In the High Street, the building on the right caught our reporter's eye. "The palatial warehouse of Macdougall & Co., of clan tartan fame, was adorned in gorgeous style," he wrote.

"Coloured shields of different designs and lovely tartan plaids set off the first storey with admirable effect. The armorial bearings of the different clans were laid out on their respective tartans, while in the centre of the second flat was the appropriate device 'Diamond Jubilee of our Beloved Queen'. ... The whole was exceedingly effective and pretty."

Jubilee decorations, Church Street

QUEEN Victoria's 60-year reign was celebrated in style, with each street trying to outdo the next in the exuberance of its decorations.

Flags and streamers, banners and bunting, crowns, shields, and portraits of the Queen were in profusion everywhere, hanging from houses, shops and offices throughout the town. Every other building was swathed in red, white and blue.

At the top of Church Street, beside the Steeple, an archway was erected proclaiming the length of the monarch's reign.

"This long thoroughfare was exceedingly gay with coloured flags, foliage, and lines of Venetian masts draped in red, white, and blue," the Courier noted.

"Altogether the general decorations of the street, which were under the charge of Mr Gall, architect, were of a beautiful character. . . . In many cases the premises were decorated in an original and expensive manner, and probably the street never presented a more handsome appearance."

Castle Street in 1897

PREPARATIONS for the Diamond Jubilee celebrations were apparently still in progress when the photographer recorded this Castle Street scene for posterity.

A handful of bystanders are taking an interest in what is happening outside the Town House — perhaps the finishing touches were being put to the wooden barrier which would soon be needed to stop a crowd of over 1000 patriotic Invernessians swamping the Exchange at the official ceremony.

"On looking into Castle Street from the Exchange the view was picturesque and striking," observed our Jubilee correspondent.

"Here the Venetian masts stretch midway up the street, and with the festoons and bunting profusely distributed along the line, together with the handsome and well-arranged productions of private enterprise, a picture was produced that won general commendation. . . . With several streamers crossing at intervals an effect was produced that was most creditable and praiseworthy."

Union Street

ON her Diamond Jubilee, Inverness went to enormous lengths to demonstrate its loyalty to "Victoria the Good", the aged and revered monarch who personified an Empire on which the sun could never set.

These townsfolk are admiring the decorations in Union Street — "our most imposing thoroughfare", according to the Courier — and in particular the store on the left, now occupied by Arnotts.

"The extensive and handsome warehouse of Messrs A. Fraser and Co., house furnishers and decorators, was the most gorgeously and artistically embellished show in town," it was reported.

"Notwithstanding the fact that the large staff employed by the firm were busily engaged at the decorations, time was found to make a show which was admired by thousands of spectators during the day." For beauty of design, effectiveness of arrangement, and general artistic charm, Union Street was "unanimously awarded the palm".

Jubilee ceremony at The Exchange

A VAST crowd gathered at The Exchange for the town's formal civic tribute to Queen Victoria on her Diamond Jubilee.

"The demonstration as a whole evoked unbounded enthusiasm, and the cheering sent up by the great gathering was loud and long," the Courier observed.

"The singing for the most part was excellent, and in patriotic passages rose to an inspiring strain."

They even tried to sing the National Anthem in Gaelic, although "most of the people present did not know the language, and had recourse to the useful phonetic print which was included in the programme."

It was noted with disapproval, however, that many men did not remove their hats.

"It seemed that the Anthem did not carry completely over the vast crowds," suggested our reporter. "At all events, it was hardly possible to doubt their loyalty, for one feeling pervaded all classes."

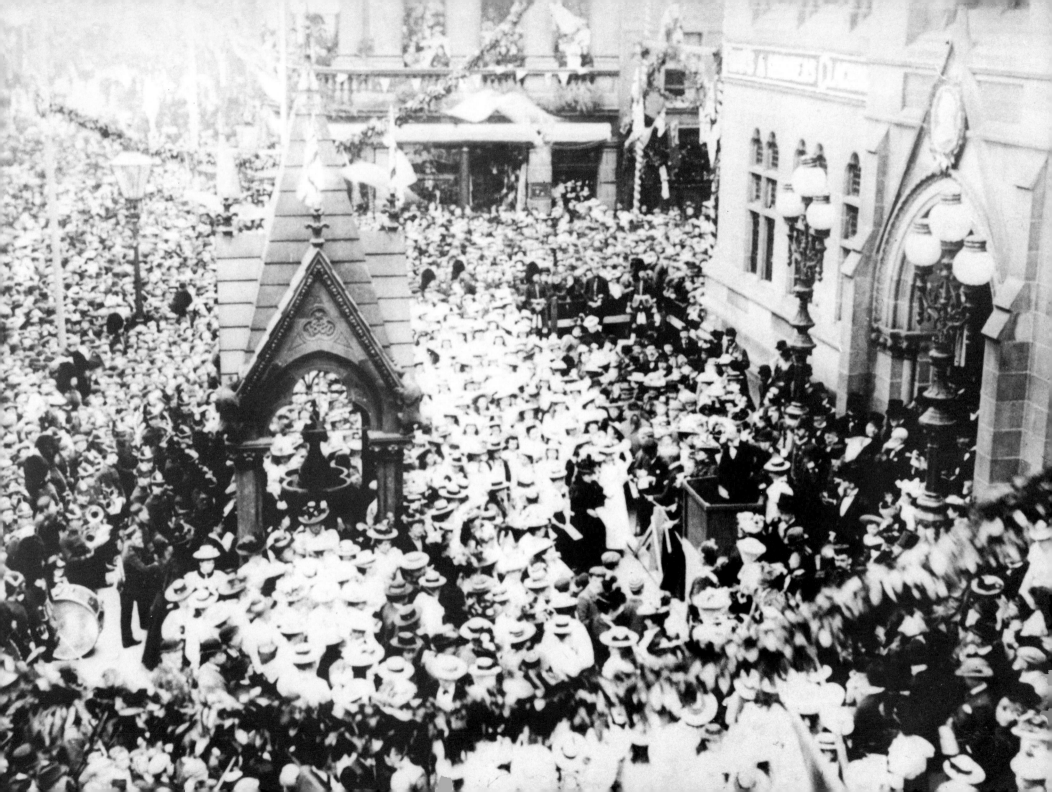

Lloyd George

JUST a section of the huge crowd which gathered at the Exchange to see Lloyd George and his Ministers arrive at the Town House for their historic Cabinet meeting in September 1921.

The Prime Minister, on holiday in Gairloch, had called the meeting to discuss the mounting crisis in Ireland after De Valera's rejection of Dominion status within the Empire.

"Overhead all the windows and coigns of vantage, on roofs and chimney-heads, were occupied by spectators, the female sex probably having the majority," the Courier reported.

There were cheers for Lloyd George and Winston Churchill, then Colonial Secretary, but the rest of the Cabinet went largely unrecognised in that pre-television age.

"The arrivals of these distinguished men were practically unmarked for the simple reason that they were not identified by the spectators," our reporter explained.

The picture also shows just how narrow Bridge Street was in those days.

Cabinet meeting

NOT even the presence of the Prime Minister could dislodge Provost Donald MacDonald from the civic chair for this historic photograph of the Cabinet members who met in the Council Chamber on September 7th, 1921.

A sombre-looking Lloyd George (centre left) was in Wester Ross when emissaries from Sinn Fein brought news of Ireland's rejection of King and Empire.

Five other Ministers were also on holiday in Scotland, and King George V was at Moy Hall.

They could all have returned south to discuss the crisis, but the Welsh-speaking Premier opted to remain among his "brother Celts" to debate the future of Ireland.

The Courier's London correspondent was in no doubt Inverness was a deliberate choice, calculated to "appeal to the Irish imagination" rather more than Downing Street.

The Cabinet, including future Prime Ministers Stanley Baldwin and Winston Churchill, signed their names to a paper, a copy of which still hangs in the Chamber.

Culloden Cairn

CULLODEN Battlefield became increasingly popular with Victorian tourists, and during the summer MacRae & Dick ran regular coach excursions from Inverness in this four-in-hand.

It left Station Square every Tuesday, Thursday and Saturday morning, and also visited the Castles of Kilravock and Cawdor.

This publicity picture appeared in an advertisement of 1894 when the fare was six shillings return, or seven-and-six for a box seat.

The Cairn was erected in 1881 by the last resident laird of Culloden, Duncan Forbes, at the same time as the stones marking the graves of the clans.

Some of these graves were disturbed when the road was driven through the battlefield. This was a brutal act, in the Courier's view, and we were "glad to rest in ignorance of the irreverent wretch who planned it."

Only in recent years has the road been re-routed, the trees felled, and the field of battle restored to what it was.

King's Stables

THESE thatched cottages to the west of Culloden Battlefield are said to date from the time of the battle, and were still family homes when the picture was taken in the 1880s or 90s.

The one on the left, known as King's Stables Cottage, was presented to the National Trust for Scotland in 1944 and after some years as a visitor centre it is now used as a store.

It was inhabited until just after the turn of the century, and one visitor remembered: "It was always a snug little place with wooden rafters, a clay floor, and an open fireplace."

The name recalls Stable Hollow, further to the east, where the Duke of Cumberland's dragoons were based while guarding the area for some days after the battle.

Tradition has it that the seed of the ragwort, a common weed locally, was introduced with the hay brought in to feed the horses.

Cumberland Stone

BARE feet were the order of the day for most children in the Victorian era, and these youngsters from the 1880s were no exception

They are squinting at the camera from a vantage point on the Cumberland Stone, from which the Duke of Cumberland is said to have surveyed the progress of the Battle of Culloden in 1746.

Of the 12 children pictured, perhaps on a Sunday School outing, only one has boots on her feet — and she has been given centre stage.

The Duke was on horseback for most of the 40-minute conflict, in the midst of the Hanoverian lines. But there is a tradition that, at some time during the day, he stood on this stone to survey the situation and may have eaten a hasty meal upon it.

Field Marshal Lord Roberts visited the battlefield in 1903 and declared the stone was "an admirable position from which to see the country."

Kessock sailing ferry

THE Kessock Ferry in the days of sail, when the crossing could take 20 minutes or half an hour depending on the state of wind and tide.

"In a calm, the oars were resorted to, and the clocks on either side were not at all in sympathy with the arrival and departure of the boats," recalled Joseph Cook.

This picture dates from 1896, just two years after the worst disaster in the history of the ferry service had claimed the lives of six men.

One stormy February night the boat was crossing with supplies to the south pier when she began to sink, and skipper Murdo Macleod sounded the distress horn.

In darkness and blinding sleet, the South Kessock coastguards set out to the rescue in a small rowing boat. Somehow they managed to pick up the ferrymen, but then their own boat capsized. Only two men survived the tragedy, which left five widows and 26 fatherless children.

Kessock steam ferry

THE steam boats Nellie and Maud plied the Kessock Ferry before, during and just after the First World War.

They were named after the grandmother and aunt of the present Lord Burton of Dochfour, whose family owned the Kessock estate and ferry rights at one time.

Here, the Nellie is chugging gently in to South Kessock pier.

A trip across the ferry was a favourite summer outing for Inverness families but, in the winter, passengers were often outnumbered by cattle, sheep or pigs on their way to market.

For the children it was a great adventure — the skipper in his peaked naval cap, the deck-hands puffing their pipes as they slipped the moorings, and the engineer, covered in coal dust, clutching an oily rag to mop his burnished brow.

"The smell was exquisite," one of them later recalled. "A mixture of seaware, coal smoke, steam, oil, and a whiff of bogie roll."

The White House

THIS two-storey thatched house stood on what is now Thornbush Road, just beyond the railway bridge at the end of Lower Kessock Street.

It was usually whitewashed and became a prominent landmark on the route into town from the Kessock Ferry.

Travellers took their bearings from "The White House", and in due course their well-beaten path became a proper road.

That may explain why the road passed so close to the corner of the building that its gable end jutted out onto the pavement.

Joseph Cook remembered it belonging to a local solicitor called Forbes, but in the 1840s it was the home of Mr Maclennan, secretary of the Fishermen's and Mariners' Society.

In the field opposite, near the Grant Street Park, the first sod was cut for the railway line to the north in 1860.

The White House was demolished in the 1930s to permit the widening of India Street.

Salmon netting

SALMON fishermen at Carnarc Point, South Kessock, setting their nets at the mouth of the River Ness in the early years of this century.

The fishing rights on the river date back to the creation of Inverness as a Royal Burgh in the 12th century, and were confirmed by King James VI in the "Golden Charter" of 1591. This bestowed on the burgh the right to take salmon from "all and haill the water of Ness", from the Clachnahagaig Stone, near Holm Mills, "even unto the sea".

By the 19th century most of the fishing was leased to commercial operators who made a successful living from salmon netting and established a flourishing export trade.

In earlier times salmon cruives, or traps, were built at the Ness Islands and their remains can still be seen. Poaching salmon from the river was a heinous offence, and offenders were liable to be "luggit", or nailed by the ear, to the Tron.

Charleston, North Kessock

SINCE the opening of the Kessock Bridge, the village of North Kessock and its "suburb" of Charleston, have become a rapidly expanding part of the Inverness commuter belt.

North Kessock was established by Sir William Fettes (1750-1836), the laird of Redcastle, who built the inn and old stone pier around 1828. He was also the founder of Fettes College in Edinburgh.

Originally it was simply called Kessock, a name said to derive from the Celtic Saint Kessog. The prefix North came later, to distinguish it from the south ferry terminus.

Charleston seems to be older and was founded as a fishing village in the early 1800s by Kenneth Stewart. It was named after Charles Mackenzie, the Laird of Kilcoy, who died in 1813.

Some of the old fisher cottages have survived but the smiddy and the old mill — once renowned for the quality of its oatmeal — have now gone.

Kilmuir, Black Isle

THE picturesque village of Kilmuir takes its name from the near-by church, dedicated to the Virgin Mary, which was the centre of the old parish of Kilmuir Wester until it was combined with Suddie in 1756.

Kilmuir Church, which is thought to date from the 15th century, has long been a ruin. Only the north-east and south-west gables remain, but at the east end is the burial vault of a local family, the Grahams of Drynie.

Although less than two miles from Kessock as the crow flies, Kilmuir lies at the end of a long and twisting road around the back of Ord Hill. It has thereby retained its air of seclusion, despite the inexorable growth of commuter housing in the Black Isle.

On the summit of Ord Hill (633ft) are the ruined walls of an extensive hill fort. The remains of the stone ramparts, originally laced with timber, reveal traces of vitrification.